Lost in Translation

Melissa Liberatore

BookLeaf Publishing

Presentation by *BookLeaf Publishing*

Web: www.bookleafpub.com

E-mail: info@bookleafpub.com

ISBN: 9789357743891

First edition 2023

I dedicate this collection of poems to Tom. Thank you for believing in me and for encouraging me to grow in my writing and in life.

Your Last Breath

The light was dim
and although noise permeated
through the room,
I could only hear gasps
Dualing banjos,
you and your dog side by side
A competition--who could hold their
breath the longest
I watched as the last bit of air
unraveled from your body
A little shimmy--your body rising briefly
one last time, then slowly deflating
all the way down
Your soul shaking itself free
"Your tears are my tears,"
Your words echoed in my mind
as they streamed down my face
So much held in one moment
Just hanging there--
Waiting
Keeping my breath prisoner
For what?!
Whether I hold it in or let it out
Your fate remains the same
"I love you more," I whispered

In A Loop

Am I just a character in a book
 in a language nobody else can read?
 I've been through these chapters before
 but this feels like a 2nd edition unabridged
 detailed--full of character development.
 I'm ready to get beyond these passages
plunge into the rest of the story.
 I'm so nauseous from re-reading the same
paragraphs over and over
 looking for clues
 how I could have
 should have
 would have
 long to

Expectations Of My Lover

You are the one I left my glass slipper behind for
 That you might find me again--a diamond in the
rough
 You're my beast--burdened, beautiful heart
 Held captive by an envious witch's spell
 You are my magic carpet ride--so ready to see
the world with you
 My handsome prince charming--lips magical,
awakening me from this sleepy state of existing
 Strong and sturdy prince--pluck me from the
sea
 hold me steady so I could walk on two feet
 My Flynn Rider--demanding me to let my hair
down --my ride or die... I'd rather sink my teeth
into the poisoned apple than live one moment
without you
 You--me--our own happily ever after

Eruption

This fuck it bucket is getting full
Soon it will overflow and all the
Fucks I've given over time will spill out
A volcano of compassion, empathy
Sympathy, grief, respect
All oozing along nipping at my ankles
As I flee from myself--
from the character flaws that made me
Sprinting from the fucks that I so
Generously flung around
Sprinkling them about like salt
Trying to season the potential in others
It's not safe here anymore
And there's no place to hide

The Simple Things

Deep belly laughs
 The kind where you almost
 Hold your breath
 Silent hysterical warmth
 Shooting through your body
 Any eye contact sends
 You deeper into the fit
 Face hurts
 Smiles that spread
 So wide--beaming
 Playful pillow fights
 Loving hugs
 So grateful
 Especially for the
 "I love you, Mom"

Just One More

Time, an arbitrary confinement
keeping us in check
Measuring our existence
moment to moment
Deciding how long we get to linger
How quickly moments escape us
Leaving only memories and longing
More kisses, longer hugs, endless laughter
Time has the upper hand
Keeping us yearning
for just one more minute
Pining for moments already past

Squirrling Around

They do this dance
 running circles around
 one another in the grass
 back and forth
 up the tree
 down the tree
 a tango to and fro
 stop...wait...there they go
 she slows a bit to give him a chance
 All this squirrling around
 just to get some ass

Please, Set This House On Fire

My mind is a house
locked from the outside
I pace across the living room
down the halls and back again
peer out the windows hoping
for some glimmer of peace
nothing out there
just pitch black silence
I want to be out there
floating in empty space
free from the tangled web of noise
that haunts this house
buried in the darkness
far out of reach from the neon
abstract paintings--racing thoughts
streaking in bold color across my
ability to reason
to give a shit
somebody please
set this house on fire
and let my embers float tranquilly
out into the night

Who Needs Chocolate?

There is little that competes
 With the delicious morsel that is you
 The candied taste of your lips
 Melting against mine
 The warm fuzzy hit of sugar
 That is your touch
 You are the treat I crave
 To satisfy this sweet tooth
 My very own personal stash
 Of decadent dessert

Not Up To Dick

I've got the morbs
 as the Victorians would say
 I'm missing you
 and the only logical thing to do
 is get as tight as a boiled owl
 while I'm not up to dick
 wallowing, pining
 listening to old messages
 just to hear your voice
 sifting through photos
 not being able to focus
 day dreaming about
 your sauce-box on mine

A Quest In And Out Of The Grey Areas

Life is a quest through chaos
 Weaving in and out of sunshine
 And darkness, pausing sometimes
 In the grey areas.
 It takes a while, but you learn
 That you are never stagnant--
 Stuck in one place, one mood,
 Serving one purpose.
 You're always one decision away
 From turning the table
 And pivoting in a new direction
 Eventually you understand that
 It's not the destination that is so important
 It's the journey and who you choose
 To share it with

My Attempt At Washing You Away

I stood in the pouring rain this morning
Let the drops shower down on me
That they may rinse the pain
Of missing you away
I closed my eyes and tried to be still
Letting the calamity in my brain
Tunnel around me--cool drops
Rolling down my skin
Washing away nothing
I feel you, our connection
I will never stop missing you
Deep breaths
Both feet on the ground

Escapism

She sees herself in the reflection on the water
Her eyes, stars beaming back at her
The dark sky, a monument
To the void that is her heart
Everywhere she goes, her baggage follows
She's invited it in to unpack
And take up space in her mind
Leaving her longing to run away from home

I Am A Desert

I am a desert
Its building
The tears behind my eyes
Slowly peaking
Dam breaking heights
Dry--unable to release
Holding my breathe
Frozen
Playing opossum
A sea of sand ahead
Squinting ...hoping
Crawling my way back
To the depths of the
Ocean we were born in

The Loss Of Naivety

Young
 full of adventure
 warning signs unnoticed
 caution, a foreign ritual
 she dove head first
 into freedom
 embracing each moment
 savoring sounds, sights, smells
 absorbing each new experience
 naive and eager
 to see the good deed
 waiting inside everyone
 not in tune with her intuition
 she missed the signs screaming
 DANGER
 she took his hand
 trusting in good intentions
 but she left with
 less
 and yet more than
 she came with

There Is No Good Time For Death

There is no good time for death
 but it comes uninvited nonetheless
In the middle of the night
 or the early hours of morning
 leaving you out of breath
 pushing you to self pity
 embracing your flesh
There is no good time for death
 but it pounces without warning
 no indication in sight
 Sometimes it lingers taking its time
 other time it sneaks in leaving no sign
There is no good time for death
 but it must come nonetheless

The Moon

How it exposes all its flaws
 sometimes leans in so we
can have a better look
How it washes waves
of emotions over me
everything crashing
The raw power--
an ocean for a weapon
And me, just grains of sand
being polished by the sea
The moon--omniscient
keeper of secrets
cascading over your silhouette
softly highlighting your face

Pining For Greener Grass

Why is it we strive endlessly to touch
 what is beyond our reach
No longer satisfied with what we have already
achieved
 Hungry, always,for the next best thing
 Ready to trade in all the chips
 to feel the blades upon our feet
 in hopes that greener grass
 will make us complete

Big Heads

We all know one or two
the ones who measure--
calculate everything they do
As long as they get pleasure
and at another's expense
Quite deliberate, no fault of ignorance
They use whoever will allow it
without regard for consequence
Smearing names into shit
Trudging along, stepping on heads
Their obnoxious arrogance
takes over, expands--spreads
As they grow in malicious confidence
We can only hope that their
oversized heads explode

She's A Pistol

She's a pistol they say
 Just a polite way
 to say she's a bitch
 Pushy, demanding
 The type that wants
 her cake and to eat it too
 Maybe her pride is what
 she should be swallowing
 So loud and proud
 She preaches independence--
 Girl Power!
 And yet, a walking contradiction
 expecting to be waited on
 hand and foot
 An Empress
 not wanting for anything
 So full of herself
 there isn't room for him anyway

The Point That Is Now

In this moment I reflect
 upon the difference of who
I am
Was
Could be
Who I've been demanded to resemble
Looking ahead
Leaving this moment
So busy
Avoiding this moment
I'm missing the point
That is
Now